TOO BUSY to be CREATIVE?

But wouldn't you love to ...
make a special gift for a friend ...
improve your home's décor ...
or just find time to "de-stress"?

The solution is in your hands!

Cross stitch collage is a revolutionary way to blend scrapbook papers, assorted embellishments, and a minimum of cross stitch into textural art compositions. It's a FAST AND FUN way to fit creativity into your busy schedule. Relax and enjoy this easy new hobby at break time, when you're on the phone, or while you're watching your favorite T.V. show. Just a minute here and there will quickly reward you with four stylish decorator sets. Each collage fits a purchased frame — no professional framing required!

Your friend loves her gift ...
your walls look fabulous ...

AND

you've discovered time for creativity!

Fun in the Sun

To GET STARTED...

you only need a few things • standard size frames • decorative paper and other embellishments • double stick tape • cross stitch fabric • embroidery floss

backgrounds - Most frames come with a piece of mat board or cardboard inside. Cover this board with your decorative papers, cutting and layering them any which way you want. You can even build your layering on the glass that comes with the frame. This works GREAT if you are adding 3-D embellishments that would flatten under the glass. Refer to the project ideas below for more details.

completing your project - Once you've stitched your designs on Aida, spritz the fabric on the wrong side with water. Iron dry to remove any wrinkles. Trim the fabric to 3 squares from the design's outer edges. Use double stick tape to adhere the fabric to white paper. Then use the double stick tape to adhere your stitched piece to the covered mat. Pop everything into the frame and hang on your wall. *It's just that easy!*

Project IDEAS:

COCKTAIL HOUR

(Photography on Back Cover)

The black accents tame the playfulness of the bold, graphic lines and bright, layered mulberry cardstock on these four fun cocktail pieces. A hole punch cuts the small circles from scraps of cardstock. The black is continued in the 5" x 7" frames.

FLOWER VASES

(Photography on pg. 3)

Purchased 8" x 10" frames with raised top mats create a shadow box effect for our vases. Cover the mats with handmade paper and attach the trimmed stitched pieces. Simplicity at its best.

ASIAN CHARACTERS

(Photography on Front Cover)

Handmade and metallic papers are layered along with fiber snippets and charms for this calming quartet. Look for frames that re-enforce the theme of your stitched pieces, like the 5" x 7" bamboo frames do here.

FUN IN THE SUN

(Photography on pg. 2)

Create your own waves by trimming mulberry cardstock in curvy, wave shapes along the edges. Glue on some sea shells or other beach mementos for some 3-D punch. Both 8" x 10" and 5" x 7" frames are just right.

General *INSTRUCTIONS*

how to read charts

Each chart is made up of a key and a gridded design where each square represents a stitch. The symbols in the key tell which floss color to use for each stitch in the chart. The following headings and symbols are given:

X — Cross Stitch
DMC — DMC color number
$^{1}/_{4}$ X — Quarter Stitch
B'ST — Backstitch
ANC. — Anchor color number
COLOR — the name given to the floss color in this chart

A square filled with a color and a symbol should be worked as a **Cross Stitch**.

A triangle with a reduced symbol should be worked as a **Quarter Stitch**.

A straight line should be worked as a **Backstitch**.

A large dot listed near the end of the key should be worked as a **French Knot**.

An oval listed near the end of the key should be worked as a **Lazy Daisy Stitch**. The chart will indicate the exact size and placement.

Sometimes the symbol for a **Cross Stitch** may be partially covered when a **Backstitch** crosses the square. Refer to the background color to determine the floss color.

how to stitch

Always work **Cross Stitches** and **Quarter Stitches** first and then add the **Backstitch**, **French Knots**, and **Lazy Daisy Stitches**.

cross stitch

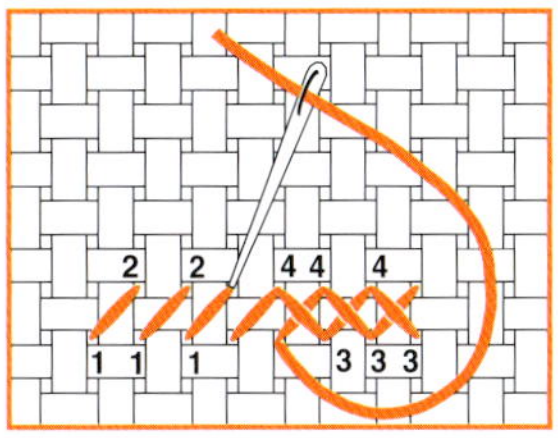

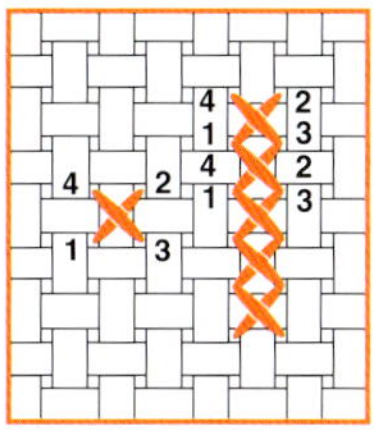

quarter stitch

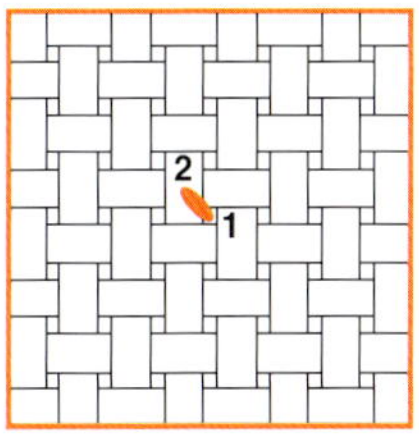

backstitch

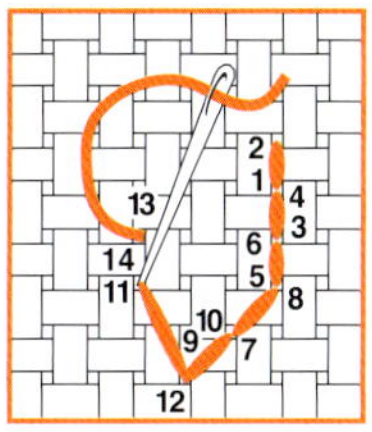

french knot

lazy daisy stitch

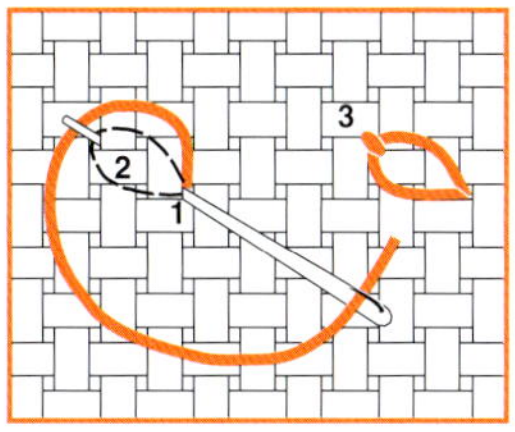

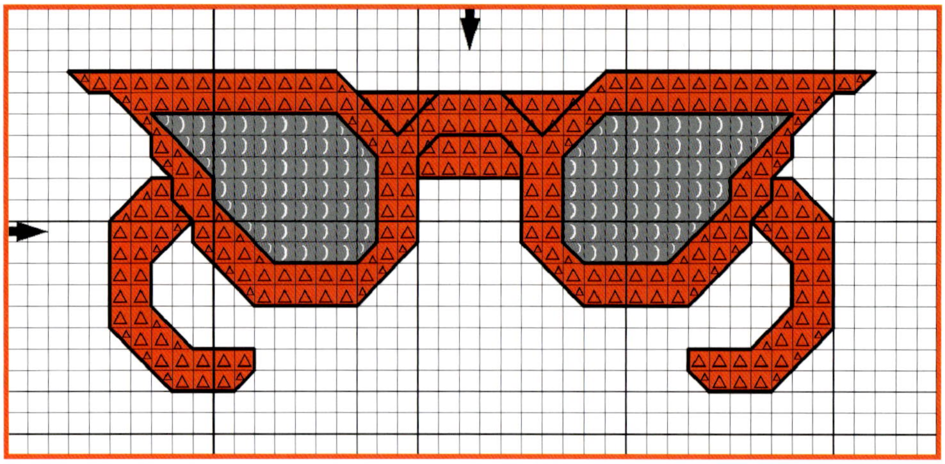

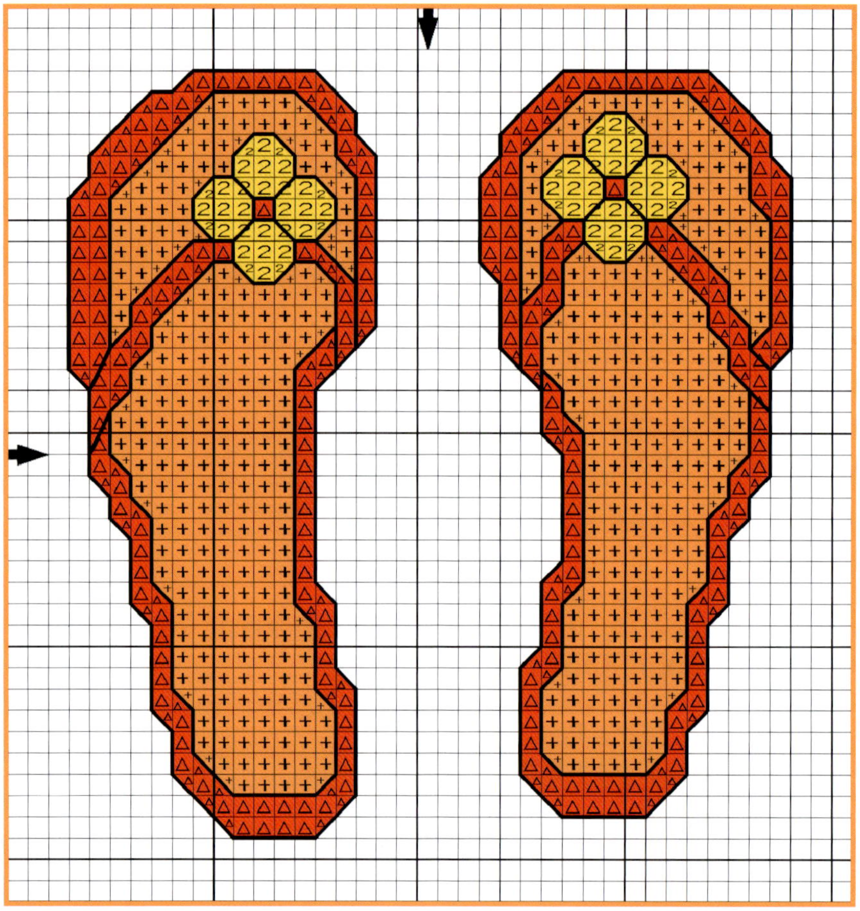

shades (39w x 15h)

flip flops (35w x 36h)

X	DMC	1/4X	B'ST	ANC.	COLOR
)	310	)	/	403	black
2	444	2		290	yellow
△	606	△		334	red
+	970	+		316	orange

shades was stitched on a 9" x 7½" piece of 14 count White Aida (design size 2⅞" x 1⅛"). **flip flops** was stitched on an 8½" x 9" piece of 14 count White Aida (design size 2½" x 2⅝"). Three strands of floss were used for Cross Stitch and 1 strand for Backstitch. See Project Ideas, pg. 4.

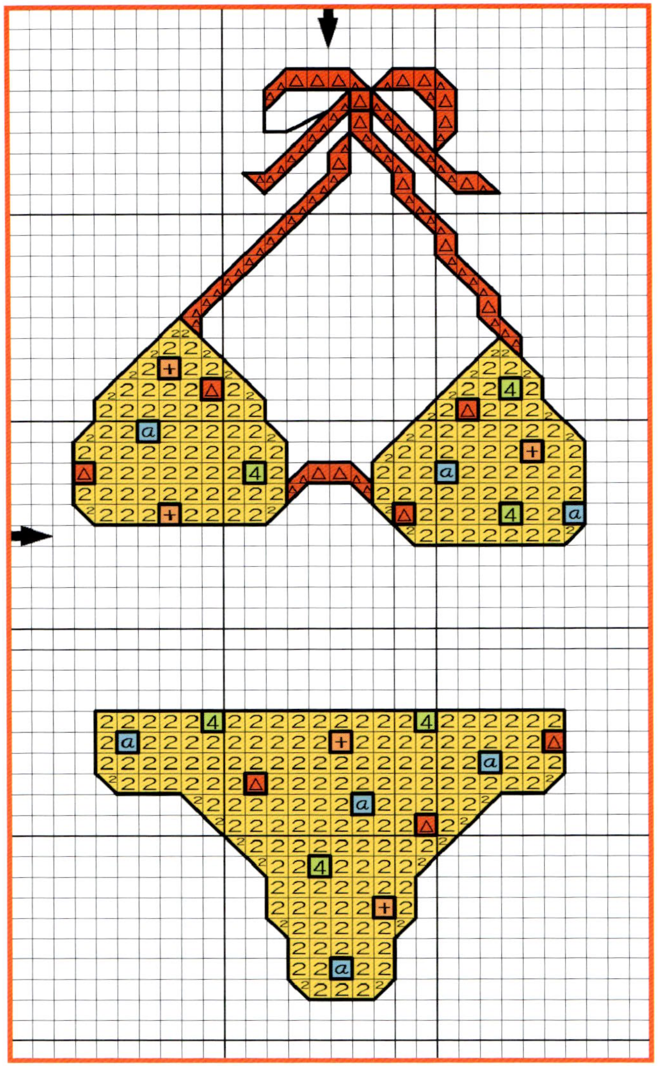

bikini (24w x 45h)

sun (38w x 39h)

X	DMC	1/4X	B'ST	ANC.	COLOR
	310		/	403	black
2	444	2		290	yellow
Δ	606	Δ		334	red
4	907			255	green
+	970	+		316	orange
a	3845			1089	blue

bikini was stitched on an 8" x 9 1/2" piece of 14 count White Aida (design size 1 3/4" x 3 1/4").
sun was stitched on a 9" x 9" piece of 14 count White Aida (design size 2 3/4" x 2 7/8"). Three strands of floss were used for Cross Stitch and 1 strand for Backstitch. See Project Ideas, pg. 4.

champagne

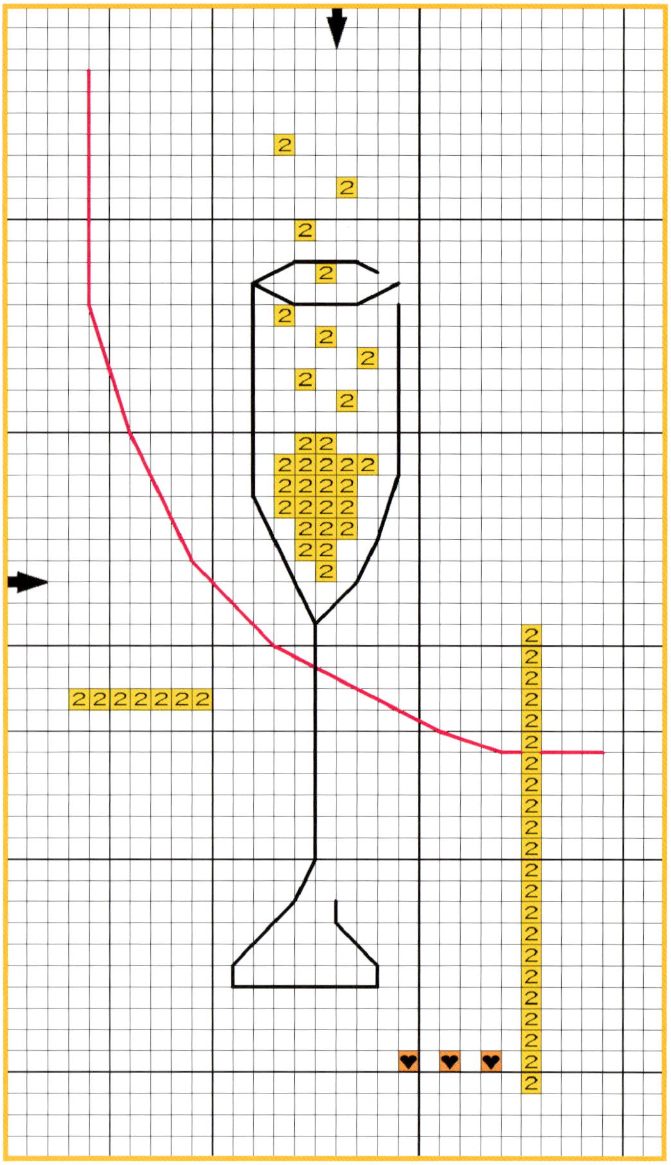

champagne (26w x 48h)

X	DMC	B'ST	ANC.	COLOR
	310	/	403	black
2	444		290	yellow
	907	/ *	255	green
♥	970		316	orange

* Use **2** strands of floss.

champagne was stitched on an 8" x $9\frac{1}{2}$" piece of 14 count White Aida (design size $1\frac{7}{8}$" x $3\frac{1}{2}$"). Three strands of floss were used for Cross Stitch and 1 strand for Backstitch except where noted in key. See Project Ideas, pg. 4.

martini

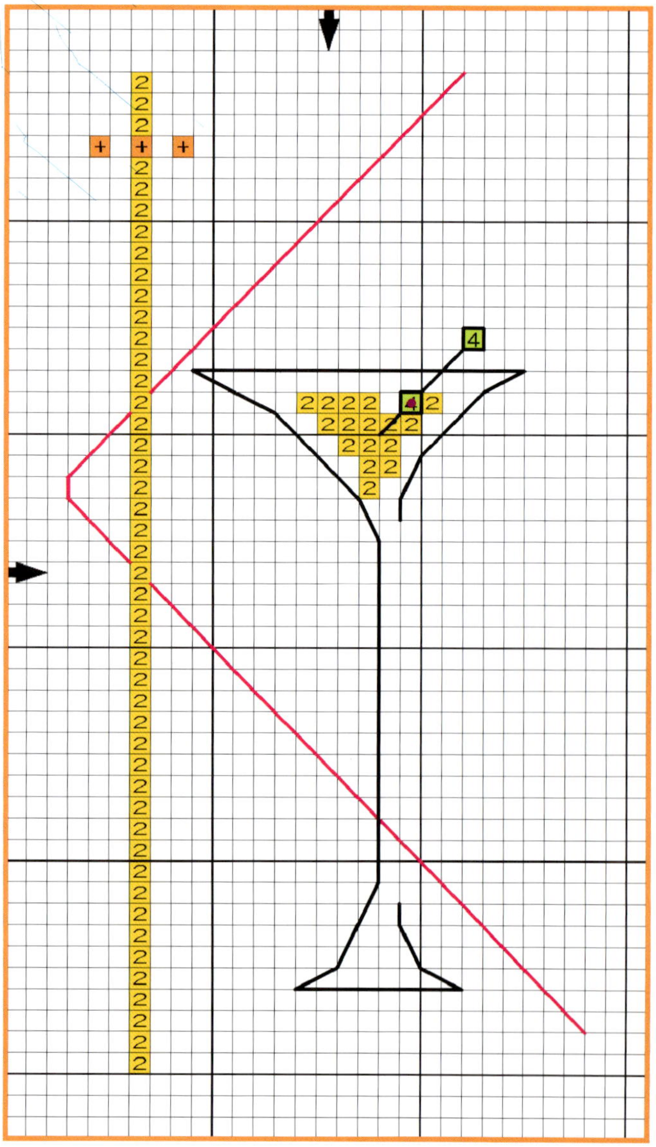

martini (25w x 47h)

X	DMC	B'ST	ANC.	COLOR
	310	/	403	black
2	444		290	yellow
4	907	/ *	255	green
+	970		316	orange
•	666		46	red Fr. Knot

* Use **2** strands of floss.

martini was stitched on an 8" x $9\frac{1}{2}$" piece of 14 count White Aida (design size $1\frac{7}{8}$" x $3\frac{1}{2}$"). Three strands of floss were used for Cross Stitch and 1 strand for Backstitch and French Knots except where noted in key. See Project Ideas, pg. 4.

tropical

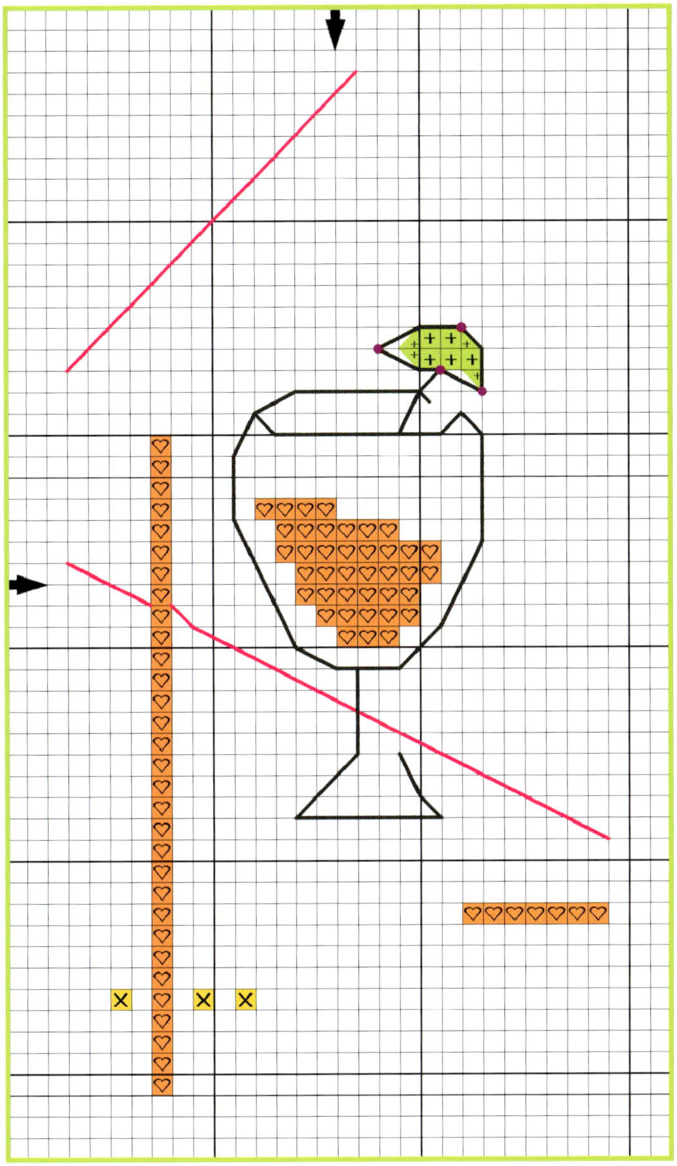

tropical (26w x 48h)

X	DMC	¼X	B'ST	ANC.	COLOR
	310		/	403	black
×	444			290	yellow
+	907	+	/*	255	green
♡	970			316	orange
•	Mill Hill Petite Glass Bead #42014 black				

* Use **2** strands of floss.

tropical was stitched on an 8" x 9½" piece of 14 count White Aida (design size 1⅞" x 3½"). Three strands of floss were used for Cross Stitch and 1 strand for Backstitch except where noted in key. See Project Ideas, pg. 4.

hurricane

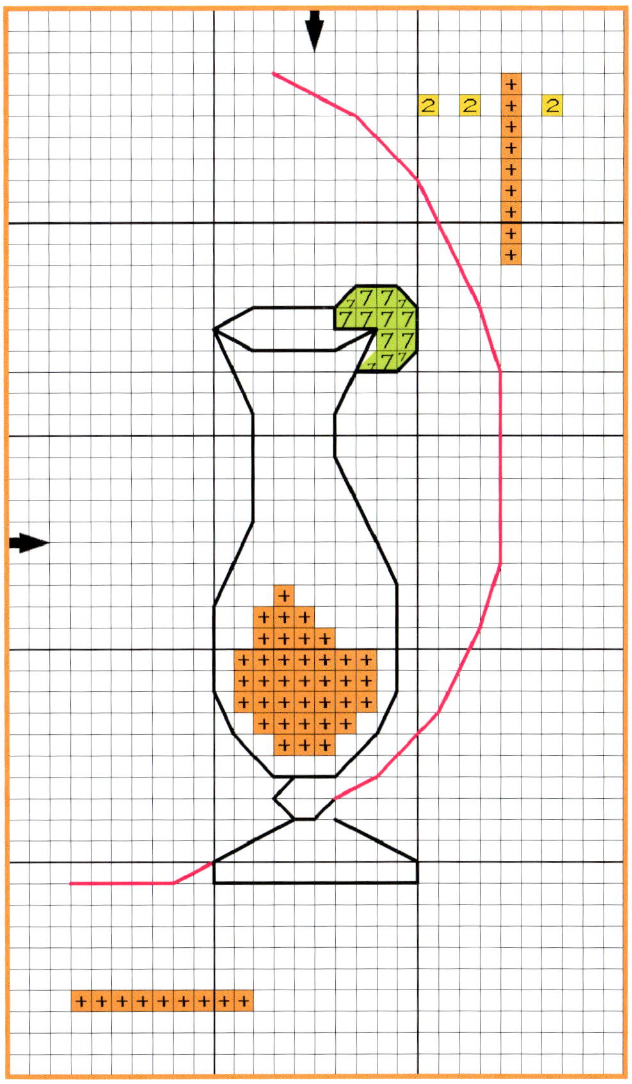

hurricane (24w x 44h)

X	DMC	¼X	B'ST	ANC.	COLOR
	310		/	403	black
2	444			290	yellow
7	907	7	/*	255	green
+	970			316	orange

* Use **2** strands of floss.

hurricane was stitched on an 8" x 9½" piece of 14 count White Aida (design size 1¾" x 3¼"). Three strands of floss were used for Cross Stitch and 1 strand for Backstitch except where noted in key. See Project Ideas, pg. 4.

happiness (41w x 47h)

X	DMC	B'ST	ANC.	COLOR
)	310	/	403	black

happiness was stitched on a 9" x 9½" piece of 14 count White Aida (design size 3" x 3⅜"). Three strands of floss were used for Cross Stitch and 1 strand for Backstitch. See Project Ideas, pg. 4.

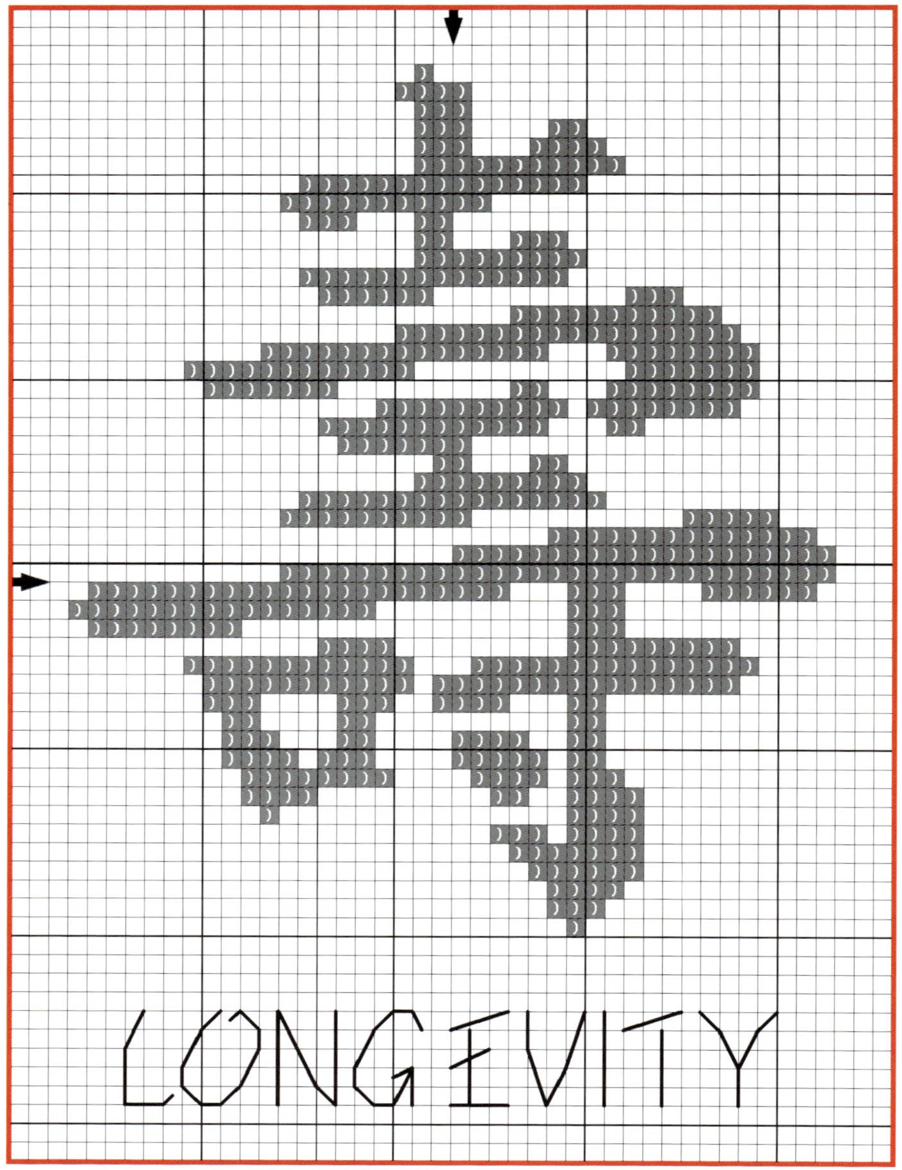

longevity (40w x 56h)

X	DMC	B'ST	ANC.	COLOR
)	310	/	403	black

longevity was stitched on a 9" x 10" piece of 14 count White Aida (design size 2⅞" x 4"). Three strands of floss were used for Cross Stitch and 1 strand for Backstitch. See Project Ideas, pg. 4.

wisdom (38w x 49h)

X	DMC	B'ST	ANC.	COLOR
)	310	/	403	black

wisdom was stitched on a 9" x 9$^1/_2$" piece of 14 count White Aida (design size 2$^3/_4$" x 3$^1/_2$"). Three strands of floss were used for Cross Stitch and 1 strand for Backstitch. See Project Ideas, pg. 4.

virtue (41w x 49h)

X	DMC	B'ST	ANC.	COLOR
)	310	/	403	black

virtue was stitched on a 9" x 9$^1/_2$" piece of 14 count White Aida (design size 3" x 3$^1/_2$"). Three strands of floss were used for Cross Stitch and 1 strand for Backstitch. See Project Ideas, pg. 4.

dahlia (13w x 44h)

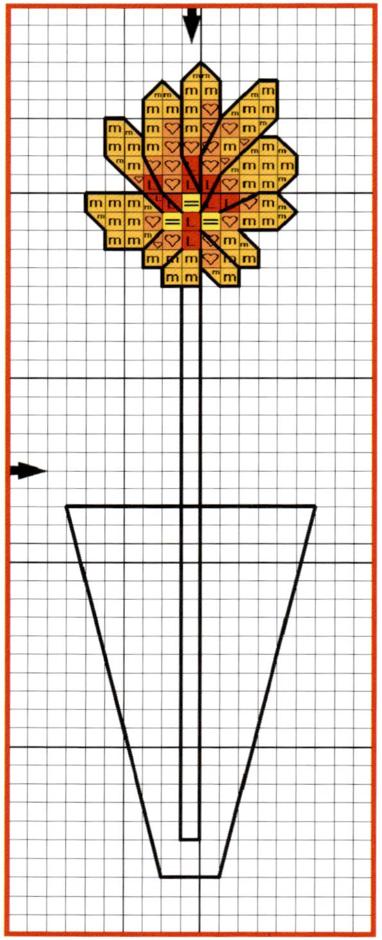

lily (16w x 45h)

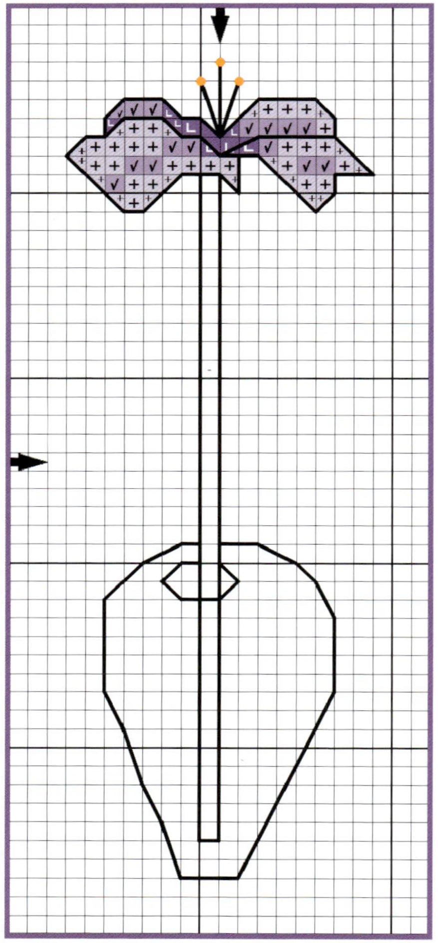

daisy (13w x 43h)

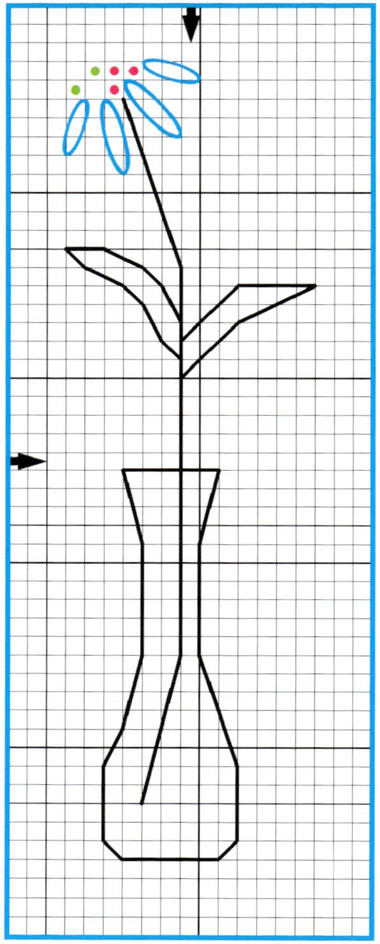

hyacinth (11w x 44h)

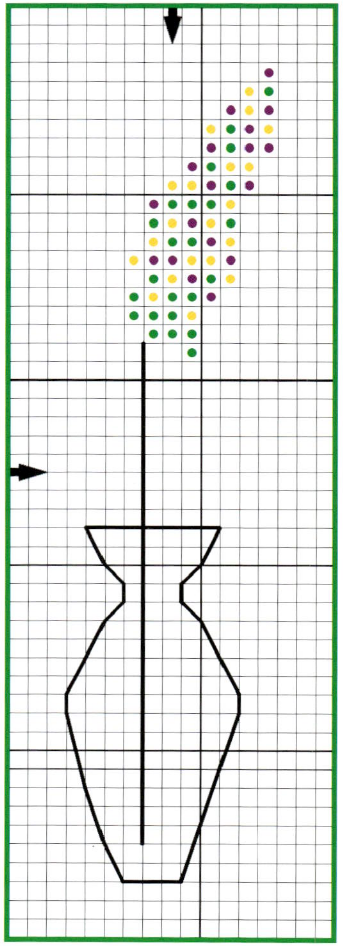

flowers

X	DMC	1/4X	B'ST	ANC.	COLOR
√	208	√		110	lavender
+	209	+		109	lt lavender
	310		/	403	black
L	550	L		102	purple
L	666	L		46	red
m	740	m		316	lt orange
=	742			303	yellow
♡	946	♡		332	orange

X	DMC	ANC.	COLOR
● *	208	110	lavender Fr. Knot
● *	209	109	lt lavender Fr. Knot
● *	310	403	black Fr. Knot
● *	740	316	lt orange Fr. Knot
● *	946	332	orange Fr. Knot
● *	3609	85	plum Fr. Knot
⊘ ★	742	303	yellow Lazy Daisy

* Use **2** strands of floss.

★ Use **3** strands of floss.

Each **flower** was stitched on a $7^{1}/_{2}$" x $9^{1}/_{2}$" piece of 14 count White Aida (approx. design size $1^{1}/_{4}$" x $3^{1}/_{4}$"). Three strands of floss were used for Cross Stitch and Lazy Daisy Stitches, 2 strands for French Knots, and 1 strand for Backstitch. See Project Ideas, pg. 4.